Fierce This Falling

Fierce This Falling

Poems by Betsy Johnson-Miller

Mayapple Press 2012

Published by   MAYAPPLE PRESS
362 Chestnut Hill Rd.
Woodstock, NY 12498
www.mayapplepress.com

ISBN 978-1-936419-12-8

ACKNOWLEDGMENTS

The author would like to thank the journals in which these poems
first appeared:

5 a.m.: "Even a dog"
Salamander: "A little land" and "Leap, soft"
Sycamore Review: "If I Were Zen"
Good Foot: "The carp, ugly"
DMQ Review: "Dirt," "along field," and "A Lost Gospel of Eve"
Lake Effect: "My grandmother and her older sisters taught me to
Sugar Step on the red brick patio in the dark"
Switched-On Gutenberg: "Concubine"
Cottonwood: "[And she dances]"
Praxilla: "Conversations from a Marriage"

Cover art by Rachel Melis. Cover designed by Judith Kerman. Book designed
and typeset by Amee Schmidt with titles in Centaur and text in Californian
FB. Author photo courtesy of Shane Miller.

Contents

Part Four: Some green saint

—for my father

The punishment for doubt
is doubt—my father's death taught me that.
                    —Ellen Bryant Voigt

Part One:
Something older than faith

After My Father's Diagnosis

You have my attention.

I am not in the valley
but there is a shadow.

I live on a hill–
how do I feel
a leviathan here?

In the Gospel
of Thomas

You told me to split open
a piece of wood.

There I would find
You.

I go down to the woodpile
and seek the biggest log.

Chopping it open I see
splinters and knots
wooden strings and worm
trails

a hunk of dead wood
that isn't proof of the divine.

It's only a thing that used to be tall.

[Who can dwell here]

Who can dwell here
with the orange flowers

and a tenderness known
only to green grass?

Who can dwell here
where some of the strangers

I am asked to love
are two doves who so far refuse

to take up my kind offer
of building a nest in my hair?

Either they don't believe me
or they don't care

that this might help us all
stop wondering Who.

My father is in the house
dying. I am out here

facing north to cool my mind
and praying for a gift

of tongues. One for bloom.
One for tender. One willing

to speak when spoken to.

She Laments

—Reading Isaiah 40

Speak tenderly the hard.

Not that you have to.
In my desert I am used to chewing sand.
My mouth tastes like mountain.

The glory of together withers
and no flowers fall from my mouth.

Life has a hollow hand and so many days

I drop.

Away from your aggravating fire.

The carp, ugly

and leg-long

in the pond

assure her

she will not enter

the water no matter

the assembling of summer

fire. Small congregations

of geese spend the morning

beseeching a world

beneath the water's surface.

When that fails

something older than faith

tells them to use their heads,

the only fists they have.

Swell

1.

what disturbs me

2.

about the slug
is its shame-

3.

less flaunting of its soft body like how a man
I know just had to have

4.

half his skull removed to let the swell of his brain
subside

after a stroke
at 38 and how

5.

dare a creature choose to live
unprotected from the simple
things like shoe, salt
or beer

6.

the man? without a skull
he must be having a hard time

7.

or rather I'm the one having a hard time
keeping my thoughts to myself

Stupid: especially due to a lack of meaning or sense

—Webster's

Living lately on my knees,
it feels perverse

this waiting for crumbs
from the universe.

I am a beggar of some Source
my husband does not believe in

(which is why, of course,
he's happy).

*

If Heaven resides in sky,
then it must be

nothing but Weather
on an ornery dumb donkey

riding by.

*

This week the frozen lakes
have been skinned—raw wet flesh

suddenly open to the wind.

*

It's been said rain is Heaven
crying. I'm here to tell you:
Heaven is sitting on its ass.

It isn't even trying.

God Answers

—Reading Isaiah 41

I am Fathom. I am Worm.
I reach my arms to the deep.
I open the dirty.

I know the thirsty search
for water but when I present you river
when I declare you filled
you stir the sun
with your tongue.

Fine. Uphold your rage.
Harvest the hard mountain,
bake it crushed into your bread,

but then quit seeking
to be carried with the first
and the last.

I took you from the corner.
Do not think you can dismay me
with your fear.

Do you hear?
Do something awful.
I still choose you.

The rock is right

down there at the bottom of our hill.

It can see the sky only when the leaves

are gone and snow ruins even that sometimes.

The rock—without flesh, bone—might be glad

for death to come to sparrow or rabbit.

To see hardness steal into a body. To watch

the living move to quite dead. And master

dead quiet.

November, 2008

You and I do not mark the moon
and her pale phases, but at the dwindling
of my father's body, we can't
stop our silent gazes.

I hold my mother and her misery
and then under nightly slide
of moon hide in your arms.
I cannot stop grief or want

so I will stay with what love
can do—arrive in our bed late at night
or disappear. Like my father's breath
and the half-eaten heart of the moon.

What If Winter Is My Buddha

I concentrate

on envy,
for those who are free

of winter
are surely at peace.

Holding onto winter
like a hot coal, intent
on throwing it at someone else,

I am not about
to have compassion
for winter—even if each
winter has its own suffering—

I am not about to discover
my winter and then—
with all my heart—give
myself over to it.

"Are you awake?" my husband asks.

"No. I am winter."

Even a dog

Still in the dark I try
to tell if I am numbered with the damned,
who cry, outraged, Lord, when did we see you?
—Jane Kenyon

This God of air
but not dirt
hides in the number
of hairs
on a head
balances angels
on a pin.

This God
who's chosen
silence
wishes we
would do the same.

My God
even a dog
comes when it hears something

and it doesn't have to be weeping.

Corn in the birdfeeders

When the ragtag infantry
of winter light
limps across the last leg of sky,

when the dog attacks
the window because the hungry
pheasant dares approach,

when the woman reaches
into the cupboard to feed on the dark
chocolate,

then winter takes the field
and turns the battle.
Just ask the deer

staring at the house
her skin holding life
like a corset: keep it in,

keep it in.

Don't be afraid to say, "O God,
you are so good to me."

—advice from a nun

If You said that thing
about *Good*

and *Let there be lightness*

why must You be so penny
something I don't care if I lose

something I leave behind in gas stations
seven states away

why do You have to be so bone
all hidden and hardness

something I can't see
till I'm hurt and gaping

I'll bet You like that idea—
bone

what all that I am
is meant to hang onto

A Lost Gospel of Eve

Okay. Naked.

And the guy.

I get the outcome of fall.

All it sorrowed.

We work.

From when the left sky is shining.

To a dark dark.

I don't mind that.

It's the turn of his face now.

And his back.

It's all this earth.

I have a feeling it wants.

Whatever is living.

Inside me.

Part Two:
Fierce this falling

funeral is to snow

it snows real

it whites all the way

wind bears no mention of spring

fierce this
                      falling

the sky offers a cold peace

a measurable presence

we have a word for this:

buried

Such an Eye That Could Behold

I. The Life Cycle

The turtle isn't so much dead as puzzled by time and rain,
its shell reduced to shingles.

Vertebrae pile in whittled scraps.
They might have been whistles.

My children found the turtle two days ago under deadfall. Budding
biologists they asked for the blue blanket we use on picnics.

My dogs circle the blanket as I eat my lunch on the deck today.
Only my salami sandwich gets more attention.

Deer and weasel, pheasant and fox. We can get close
only when fight and flight are impossible.

My children carried these bones,
delighted. Dancing.

II. January Manifesto

Children of the summer turtle unite
in patience and in cowardice
waiting long and without a fight
always ready to disappear.

Kiss is what lovebirds do in trees
but not around here. It's too cold
for such afternoon affection. Seas
oh I long for a sea whose old

body still gets up every time
it falls hard upon the sand.
Lone eagle rides on air to climb
above the world and Someone planned

to give it such an eye that could behold
from its height my arms—small and up and cold.

III. If she had a tongue like mine

I am not alone in staring at the dead.
Those who woke early to gather shells

gather round the loggerhead. She traveled roads
of water, arrived here dead on a roar.

I can't stop looking at her face.
She could have answered my questions

about a crushing deep
about how to live in an absence of light

but death has a habit
of frustrating wisdom.

All day long I'm pulled back to her shell.
Her evidence of broken.

Concubine

So the man seized his concubine, and put her out to them; and they
knew her, and abused her all night until the morning. And as the dawn
began to break, they let her go. And as morning appeared, the woman
came and fell down at the door of the man's house where her master was,
till it was light.

—Judges 19: 25-26

Doors that don't open
are the ones we remember.

Knock. Knock. Scratch.

She learned how full
emptiness

can feel, how a body
can tire of things

inside. No one slept that night,
not the woman,

the master, the men
or if they did, only God

(also called He) saw
and recorded it.

It would be easy to see her
as a dog, obedient

at the door

her nails the last
thing to break.

She fell. It was light.
Or the sun came round again.

along field

the land
has fallen again
into a general
calamity of white

as water flowers
into flake and dances
with the zeal
of someone set free

the last season is past
its dying and flame
so is my father

well into absence
I see this snow
as old bone now

Alzheimer's

a woman I love
is stuck

on a slow raft
of flesh

I want her to join the water
that rushes

over cliff

that beautiful kind
of exploding

really the heart

should know when to stop

A word is like a stone

You don't love me very much
if you take me to the Emergency Room

when I am having chest pains.
You should not tell the man

who put the needle in my arm
to get more blankets

because you can't stand my body
shaking like that.

You should not take my hand or the doctor's
side when she says *overnight* and *test* and *care*

and *best*. You should have carried me
to bed because then I wouldn't have been

riding in the car with that ridiculous heart
and I wouldn't have had a chance

to notice dark clouds that would soon
bark with rain.

I wouldn't have been able to cry
out, "I don't want to die!"

and you wouldn't be able to hold me
to that for the rest of my days.

What is romantic now

Three nights ago you rose
from the couch and opened
the cage to pull our son's
dying gerbil out by the tail.

I watched you as we watched tv.
You held the dying that no one
had asked you to hold
that no one else had thought

to hold. No full moon.
It wasn't even raining. Just you
stroking her body
with your square thumb.

[An owl on the dead]

An owl on the dead branch one day
perfect feathers. Wild.

I can see the branch from my window

its height–some heaven–where living things are watched
until they die.

My father died a month ago today, his body made light
by fire

so how were his ashes so heavy?

Birds are already hollow
in their bones

so when it is all over their dead are easy
to bear.

What my father could have prayed

I'm about to have a new understanding of being
grounded

so God be in my bed. No, behind my restless
as a child in church eyes.

No, God be at my head—you know I always liked it best—
or by my hand, the one

being kissed
and kissed by my wife.

I have never been one for begging but give me light.

If that can't be arranged I will have
to settle for a blanket

of grass. A blanket of snow.

Like air too close to a match

It is winter. I do not feel hot and my skin
does this sound of frozen so I should feel
solid I should feel stiff, unchanging

but I must have swallowed some night
when I slept downstairs away
from my husband's body   my mouth

must have known it was away and free
to do what it wanted and it wanted
air because air is life and life is this vital

function of not being dead and my mind
must have decided it did not want to be dead
like my father so out went my lungs to pull in

as much air as possible and now I cannot fly
but I am flighty scraping my head on the sky
and wondering how to get my feet back

to something solid and not getting so caught
up in wondering if flowers fear hands
or if rain has a good time falling

and I'll bet if my husband bent down
right now and kissed me on the forehead
I'd demand *Why'd you do that?*

Were you being funny? and he'd leave me
closing the door behind him saying
Next time I'll put a rock in her shoe.

[I do not hear rice]

I do not hear rice in this
Japanese rain (nor do I hear
holsteins in the storms back home).

This rain is the same rain.
My sadness is the same sadness,
drifting in like the mist

that arrived yesterday
as I stood at the temple
fitted like a shoe on the mountain's foot.

Shrouded in incense, I believed
that hole in the trees
was about to offer me deer

or monster who would eat me
only because that was the easiest way
to carry me to a holy place

where koi were suns in dark waters
and moss climbed trees like children.
The flowers would offer sugar to my eyes

and I would carry that sweetness
back to my house, an ocean
away. but that was yesterday.

today it is raining the same rain.
the same sadness. the same rain.

Part Three:
Light floods the floor

A marriage

If we had dogs who could lead us to the dead
parts of us

would we follow?

Would you quit working so hard
at the kitchen table

would I quit standing in the middle
of the room wondering what I should do
next?

Would we wade into the dark waters
with no ark

no promise of landing

would we hold hands?

An hour later

And maybe all evening we can watch

the stars step into our dark.

You sit in that chair while I drink

the night black. The fight is over.

Mars has left the space behind my right eye

returning to its place as a red thing

in the southern sky. It's long,

isn't it? This until death.

Three days later

Tonight the empty house
reminds me how much I love you.
You have our kids and a canoe.
You will spend the night calling
to wolves, sleeping with nothing
but thin fabric between you
and the same sky I do not go outside to see.
But it's there. Over you, over me.

Conversations from a Marriage

1. Previously, A Headache

My world is in need of translation.
No, it's not.

Really?
It's simple. Give me a breast and let me see if I can get you all the way to smile.

But joy is delicate.
No, it isn't. Come on, let me get a little song under you.

But sex would require my inner monk to get naked.
Look at Buddha. Flesh flesh.

Well, okay then.

2. Second Honeymoon in Italy

Don't point your gelato at me.
I'm glad you noticed. Want a lick?

3. Fur, Stone, Fight

I do not have enough fur.
You aren't a stone, either.

I mean I am quite naked.
I must have missed it since you're wearing clothes.

I mean my skin can hear everything.
So I'm wandering the earth with an ear?

Shut up.
I'm just trying to follow your thousand wanderings off the path.

Stone head.
    Fur face.

Evil pancake, flip away.
    Sure, I'll be your syrup.

My dinner plate is getting angry. I can't promise it will miss your head.
What are you doing?
    You're about to be the woman with an open dress.

4. Hieroglyphics for "How Was Your Day?"

Daisy. Boiling. Bee sky.
    I'll become a flower, beg you to kiss this location.

Fine. Wife I Am—Bearer of Sting.
    (I know.)

What did you say?
    Your eyes. This praise. Wanna bumble?

5. Homes Are Happier

The mirrors in other homes are happier.
    Maybe, but our dwelling could be long and good.

Look. Even the moon wasn't created to be constant.
    What about the sun?

I hate you.
    Here. I gathered this water from a storm. Drink it and be satisfied.

6. Anniversary

In loneliness I am housed.
    Every door in this house opens.

You don't hear my dreams at night.
No, only your fears.

You have to tell me why you are still here.
I'm not done with your face yet.

What does that mean?
Sometimes you smile.

I pray the crawl of green

Wet fragrance bleeds from livid
land—I can finally say good bye
to winter

but this one convinced me
I should act this life seriously

because a long cold time is coming along

and while out back
is not so much a great wood
as a few trees, if I stay small

curious, perhaps
I can find some best days right here

and be able to say along with the tulip,
I'm started

Vacation Poem #1: What she calls familiar

Her man squats on a rock
to photograph the brave
monarch warming itself
inches from the waves
of Lake Superior.

There are bones under here
she thinks and fish
the size of trees. Water so
everywhere she can't believe
there's any room left for air.

She can hardly hear because
the waves pound like a pulse,
like somebody knocking
on the door.
Somebody

wants to see her
and yes probably hold her
accountable and she prays
to a god above
because a god below—in light

of all this water—is far
too menacing. And then
he's done. Done squatting.
Done taking a picture
of the beautiful thing.

He turns toward her
and she can't believe
his eyes. How they want
to see her. How he wants
to hold her. How he wants in.

Leap, soft

You are capable of hitting her
heart from a hundred
yards away. Flesh falls
from bone, the knife
in your hand plows
it open so. You have proven it.
You could feed us for a winter
or an apocalypse. You
could save our bellies
from becoming caves.
I prefer cans. Ambiguous
packaging. You cannot touch me
until you shower. I will not kiss you
until tomorrow when you give me
a piece of her. I love her
taste—corn, leap, soft sun.
I hate you. I love you
for what you have done.

If I Were Zen

A duck leaves
water

I stop
eating.

        What color
        is that flower?

        What is color?
        That flower.

Dog
leash

chipmunk
ouch.

A little land

She keeps walking a little land

doesn't own it

can't control its fate

let alone the startled flight

of light or mice who die there.

She keeps walking. A little. Land

and sky and birds

go between. Not a doubt among them.

Without gate or door night enters

just as she makes it to the water.

Water that holds every last piece

of light but not the smallest stone.

Vacation Poem #2

Rain is rain is rain except when a storm moves
on Lake Superior and I am in the harbor

of your legs wearing the black silk negligee
you bought me last week at an antiques store

that had a kitchen table once owned
by the F. Scott Fitzgeralds, or at least

that's what the man with the pinkie ring said.
I wanted the table not the silk. I swore

I would never wear it.

This late afternoon I stood at the window
watching the storm and said,

"It's good we aren't camping
on the shore tonight," which was my way

of admitting the only way we could afford this
hotel room was because we didn't buy that table.

I pulled out the negligee you
had packed in your suitcase

and led you to the floor. Here
we sit, window watching

the lightning that stays in that sky out there.
That is, until you kiss my shoulder. Then

this certain light floods the floor of me.

My grandmother and her older sisters taught me to Sugar Step on the red brick patio in the dark

Even without music these four

sisters were back to shushing

feet and smoking lips and hoping

their mother wouldn't find out

they were back to dark

places and men's bodies

back to rhythm and what

a body could do their knees

forgot lamentation their backs practiced

resurrection and I joined them in the hope

that one night I, too, would be

called upon to teach some little

girl what it is to dance

Part Four:
Some green saint

[I'm lost on a good road.]

I'm lost on a good road.
It appears
I'm the only one here.

The road is not coy—
if I am willing
it will go on

revealing
to me
these simple facts:

there is wood
in the woods
joy in the curves

and meat in the deer.

About the After Life

Very well perhaps I am thinking

about bees even though I am dead

in the middle of winter because

thinking about bees right now

is an act of faith a sincere hope

in the intention of creation

to go on and become light again.

I'm assuming there will be flowers–

an inflation of color, a rising

from the ground. I'm assuming

I will be happy.

Dirt

If you can't find me, look somewhere

by the river. I'll be the one
listening

to bullheads swim—

the one on her back–
alfalfa, alfalfa, anoint
my soil.

With grace the sun
lands

on the hill's backbone
while crows toss

to wind
their salty words.

A summer of sweet
pieces.

Thick of green flame and row
upon row

this corn with its fingers
in the dirt.

the garden bed

certainly this dirt is dead.
even the birds proclaim it so
which means like my ex-boyfriend's
cologne I am never going to have any future
pleasure from it. sad tongue. seedlings so small
they couldn't possibly.

and then again those hands.
holding the hose squirting the ground.
you and your green bean sweet pepper fat
cabbage hope. you took rocks from here

and put them over there. it was weird. like
you were suddenly holding a club and wearing nothing
but a fur over one shoulder. man, you came to bed
and I wanted your hands more than ever
I wanted my ex-boyfriend's. I couldn't stop

my heart from going in the direction
of acre. I kept kissing. and was pleased. things.
growing large.

[And she dances]

And she dances through the streets
this girl who can't believe kites
aren't allowed

in the city but she understands buildings
don't want to share the sky
and the sky has something to do

with time though she has forgotten
that lesson. She dances
past hill, past

field, horse and bird.
Sky and more sky
as the girl makes it

all the way to a river
where she sits
and finds rocks

pulling out the glad sounds
water has carried
all along.

I grew up

in the 80s
maybe that's why
I get a case

of the holies
whenever I walk
through a stand

of oak trees
my arm hairs
rise hard

totally
like branches
and I have

this o my god
sense that
the awesome lives

in the gnarly

My recent universe

I live at the edge of things
a small town, a wet land

I live where rabbits are thankful for infidelity
to an exact route
especially when my dog is after

here sun takes off
moves round
settles in

I would say: the dusk rows across the sky
my husband: night

it's not like I give my children dew
to drink

or think now and then to give them a piece of elephant
wisdom

it's not even like I can bring myself to long lean
into my husband's kiss most nights

if you ask the birds
who arrive here every morning they'll swear
this is a house without a table

then go back to feasting

Maybe

my father wanted to be cremated
because three times a day
he cleaned everything
off his plate. He couldn't bear to leave
anything behind.

From there to here

My back takes on the coat of your body
and it should be a sin

how quickly you fall asleep
while I stay awake

nervous about how we are nothing
but fragile flesh, and car and cancer cell

both know it. You twitch on your way
to sleep. Perhaps you are rowing across a lake

its water flat and cold in this grave earth
where weeds are dark forests and docks

are high churches and fish are God's angels
who can't look anyone straight in the eye.

Six Minutes of Love

When you do arrive
four & a half minutes late
you have so many books
you can't fit them all
in your bag & as you try
I see you have this loose
skin now
        that you didn't
when we married

& I have this time
to consider your skin
because you can't
get your books in your bag

finally you manage it
we walk down
the stairs & are just about
to step outside when you stop

in front of the planted
flowering tree & ask
Is this real I say yes but
you don't believe me so you smell

one red flower & come
away with yellow pollen
on your nose

I wipe it off I touch your face
which grows out of your head
like a flower

here my real love
let me lean in and see
what I come away with

[o rock.]

o rock. you are a simple monster
and what you do with noise
makes my mouth shut.

in sun dark snow or sun
you don't emanate lots of sorry.
like I do. in bed. at parties.

you. your day after day. same.
such a great plot you.
with your heaven and earth.

I with you feel. no real
need. I can walk home now

My Daughter's 6th Grade Teacher Plays Trombone in the Driveway across the Street

Now it is April and the kitchen windows
are open so I hear the music as it begins,
right when I am putting cookies in the oven.

It's raining a little. My daughter presses her nose
against the screen door and watches him.
He keeps playing his trombone, this

teacher who reads Chomsky and closes
the classroom door when he tells the truth.
My daughter, who is in love

with Nancy Drew, deduces
he must be waiting to go fishing
with the man who lives across the street

(it helps that a fishing rod leans against
the bumper). It takes me several
minutes to recognize the song:

raindrops keep falling on my head,
and it takes me several days to recognize
the feeling: it's like a boy

I don't even know tapping my shoulder
as I put my math book away. I turn and find him
offering me a handful of tiny purple stars

that smell like lilacs.

And Grass

I confess
the day more
than I can take.

Hear
my falter.

Trees need
no armies

flowers
need no knives

but the hawk's shadow keeps this
from being neat.

I pass under that cloudless bird
in a field content
with stones.

What light.
Such bright hurt.

And grass.
Lovely it whispers.

Glossolalia.

This land. Some green
saint, living

an unintelligible life
of delight.

The Day We Are Delivered a Rodent's Manifesto

After we get the mouse
out of the cat's mouth,

I take your hand:
it's a moment.

We could be off with him.
Head south

where clouds don't stick,

so bright and blue
keep coming.

Freed from shoes and bills

we could enter the multitude.
Join the big singing.

Have you read
the obituaries lately?
People with the same
number of years are dying.

Obviously

our only choice is to undress
and get down

to our own small fur. To live
like the mouse—close to dead

and suddenly free.

About the Author

Betsy Johnson-Miller lives in Minnesota and teaches at the College of St. Benedict & St. John's University. This is her second book of poetry.

Other Recent Titles from Mayapple Press:

William Heyen, *Straight's Suite for Craig Cotter and Frank O'Hara*, 2012
    Paper, 86pp, $14.95 plus s&h
    ISBN 978-1-936419-11-1
Lydia Rosner, *The Russian Writer's Daughter*, 2012
    Paper, 104pp, $15.95 plus s&h
    ISBN 978-1-936419-10-4
John Palen, *Small Economies*, 2012
    Paper, 58pp, $13.95 plus s&h
    ISBN 978-1-936419-09-8
Susan Azar Porterfield, *Kibbe*, 2012
    Paper, 62pp, $14.95 plus s&h
    ISBN 978-1-936419-08-1
Susan Kolodny, *After the Firestorm*, 2011
    Paper, 62pp, $14.95 plus s&h
    ISBN 978-1-936419-07-4
Eleanor Lerman, *Janet Planet*, 2011
    Paper, 210pp, $16.95 plus s&h
    ISBN 978-1-936419-06-7
George Dila, *Nothing More to Tell*, 2011
    Paper, 100pp, $15.95 plus s&h
    ISBN 978-1-936419-05-0
Sophia Rivkin, *Naked Woman Listening at the Keyhole*, 2011
    Paper, 44pp, $13.95 plus s&h
    ISBN 978-1-936419-04-3
Stacie Leatherman, *Stranger Air*, 2011
    Paper, 80pp, $14.95 plus s&h
    ISBN 978-1-936419-03-6
Mary Winegarden, *The Translator's Sister*, 2011
    Paper, 86pp, $14.95 plus s&h
    ISBN 978-1-936419-02-9
Howard Schwartz, *Breathing in the Dark*, 2011
    Paper, 96pp, $15.95 (hardcover $24.95) plus s&h
    ISBN 978-1-936419-00-5 (hc 978-1-936419-01-2)
Paul Dickey, *They Say This Is How Death Came into the World*, 2011
    Paper, 78 pp, $14.95 plus s&h
    ISBN 978-0932412-997

For a complete catalog of Mayapple Press publications, please visit our website at *www.mayapplepress.com*. Books can be ordered direct from our website with secure on-line payment using PayPal, or by mail (check or money order). Or order through your local bookseller.